This journal belongs to:

....

....

THIS IS ME

a Girl's Journal

JULIE METZGER, RN, MN

Illustrations by Brooke Weeber

little bigfoot
an imprint ot sasquatch books
seattle, wa

To my most favorite people in the world—
Michael, Peter, Katie, and Emma. Your wisdom,
creativity, and love are an inspiration. —J. M.

. . . .

Manufactured in China by C&C Offset Printing Co. Ltd. Shenzhen,
Guangdong Province, in December 2018

Published by Little Bigfoot, an imprint of Sasquatch Books

LITTLE BIGFOOT with colophon is a registered
trademark of Penguin Random House LLC

23 22 21 20 19   9 8 7 6 5 4

Editor: Susan Roxborough
Project editor: Nancy W. Cortelyou
Design: Anna Goldstein
Illustrations: Brooke Weeber
Copyeditor: Diane Sepanski

ISBN: 978-1-57061-939-7

Sasquatch Books
1904 Third Avenue, Suite 710
Seattle, WA 98101 • (206) 467-4300
SasquatchBooks.com

This is a book about and for YOU—a place to explore the unique and special parts of who you are today and who you are becoming.

How you use this journal is up to you. You can skip around to find pages that feel relevant to you right now, or flip to the first page and go! Maybe you'll write in it every day or just pick it up when things happen. Your creativity and curiosity are all it takes, so jump right in!

As you make your way through the journal, you may discover ideas you want to explore further. Talking to your parents and other trusted adults is a wonderful way to continue the conversation. They want very much for this whole growing-up thing to go well for you.

Warmly,

Julie

MYSELF

Let's just be fabulously where we are and who we are.
You be you and I'll be me, today and today and today . . .

—FROM *LOVE, STARGIRL*

My full name...

What I most like to be called...

The name I sometimes wish I had...

My nicknames for myself...

Other people's nicknames for me...

My signature..

My name as a design or logo

On the next page, draw a picture or create a collage of how you see yourself TODAY.

Me

My Life Story

When I was born . . .

....
....
....
....
....
....
....
....

When I was little . . .

....
....
....
....
....
....
....
....

As I got older . . .

. . . .

. . . .

. . . .

. . . .

. . . .

. . . .

. . . .

. . . .

Now . . .

. . . .

. . . .

. . . .

. . . .

. . . .

. . . .

. . . .

. . . .

IDEA TO TRY: Telling your own story and listening to other people's stories is valuable—you can learn new things about people you thought you knew well, including yourself.

Next time you're on a car trip or sitting around with friends or family, ask everyone to tell their life story in one minute. After each person finishes, take another couple of minutes to acknowledge and celebrate their story. Notice what people chose to talk about, what you learned, and what you chose to share.

Circle the words that describe you best—and add some of your own.

Angry	Giggly	Sad
Anxious	Hilarious	Sick
Athletic	Independent	Sleepy
Boring	Interesting	Sly
Bouncy	Inventive	Small
Brave	Joyful	Sparkling
Caring	Kind	Strong
Charismatic	Loud	Sympathetic
Clever	Loyal	Talented
Competitive	Messy	Talkative
Creative	Musical	Thoughtful
Curious	Nervous	Tough
Determined	Organized	Trustworthy
Different	Polite	Unique
Dynamic	Pretty	Other words:
Energetic	Questioning	
Fierce	Quiet	
Focused	Reflective	
Friendly	Relaxed	

IDEA TO TRY: Ask a trusted friend or family member which words they would use to describe you.

My Favorite Things

Obsessions/hobbies/interests ....
....
....
....
....
....

Books ....
....
....
....
....
....

Music ....
....
....
....
....
....

Movies ....
....
....
....
....
....

TV shows ....
....
....
....
....
....

Sports ....
....
....
....
....
....

Time of day ....
....
....
....
....
....

Subjects in school ....
....
....
....
....
....

Colors

....

....

....

....

....

....

Animals

....

....

....

....

....

....

Hangout activities with my friends

....

....

....

....

....

....

Things about being a girl

....

....

....

....

....

....

Things that bring me comfort ....
....
....
....
....
....
....

Things to eat ....
....
....
....
....
....
....

Things to wear ....
....
....
....
....
....
....

Things that make me laugh ....
....
....
....
....
....
....

Uniquely Me

**Draw a picture or attach a head-to-toe photograph
of yourself on the facing page.**

» Around the outside of your picture, draw symbols that represent your favorite interests (like a basketball, a chess piece, tap shoes, knitting needles, a book, a lacrosse stick, or skis).

» Below one foot, write the name of a favorite place you like to go with your family or friends.

» Below the other foot, write the name of a place you would like to go but have never been.

» Next to one hand, write an accomplishment you're proud of.

» Next to the other hand, write something you would someday like to accomplish.

» Next to your heart, write the names of two adults other than a parent that you could go to with a problem or an important question.

» Put a star next to the part of your body you appreciate most.

» Over your middle, write three things you are thankful for in your life.

» Next to your head, write one wish you have for yourself and/or the world.

» Along the bottom, add a quotation or song lyric that expresses who you are.

What I am most looking forward to when I grow up:

What worries me most about growing up:

....
....
....
....
....
....
....
....
....
....
....
....
....
....
....
....
....
....
....
....
....
....
....
....
....
....
....
....
....
....

Future Me

What parts of your life do you hope won't change in the future?

....
....
....
....
....
....
....

Do you remember all of the things you've said you wanted to be when you grow up? Make a list of them and circle the ones that still interest you.

....
....
....
....
....
....
....
....
....
....

What does the list say about you?

....
....
....
....
....
....
....

Draw a picture or make a collage of what you imagine
you'll be doing fifteen years from now.

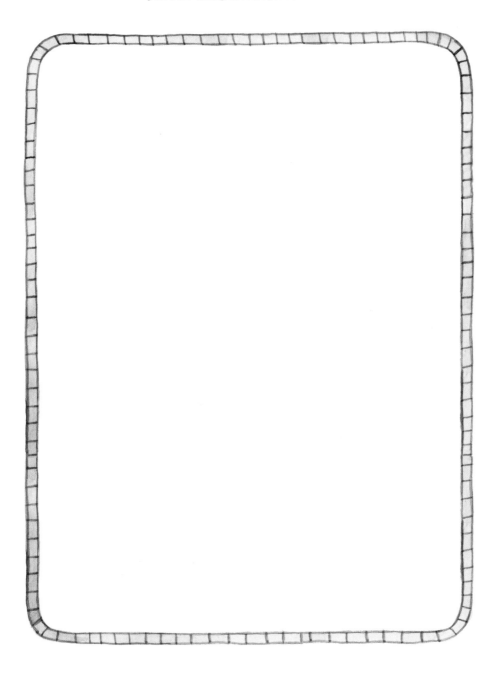

What are the things in your life that you can count on?
What are the things that make you feel settled and secure?

What things in your life make you feel unsettled and insecure?
What unanswered questions about your future bother you the most?

> **IDEA TO TRY:** When you feel uncertain, confused, or worried, make a list of all the things you feel grateful for. Reminding yourself about what is important to you can be reassuring.

Are there things you're interested in trying, or adventures you hope to have—maybe you want to learn to ride a horse, sew, speak in sign language, or climb a mountain? Challenging yourself to try something new takes imagination, courage, and hard work. Writing down your ideas can be the first step on your journey.

Things I would like to learn or adventures I would like to have:

....

....

....

....

....

....

....

....

....

....

....

What I still need to figure out:

....

....

....

....

....

....

....

....

....

....

....

....

Something that might get in the way:

....
....
....
....
....
....
....
....
....
....
....

People who can help me:

....
....
....
....
....
....
....
....
....
....
....

Have you ever imagined living an entirely different life than the one you're living right now? Maybe you've daydreamed about what your life would be like if you'd been born in another country or in another era, or if you were a superhero.

What new life would you choose, and what would it be like?

....
....
....
....
....
....
....
....
....
....
....
....

If you were a superhero, what superpower would you choose?
How would you use it?

....
....
....
....
....
....
....
....
....
....
....
....

Write about a time when you wished you were someone else or pretended to be.

You make a difference every day in people's lives and experiences just by being YOU. You change the world simply by showing up and paying attention and being yourself.

What do you consider to be your greatest gifts, talents, and strengths?

What qualities do you love most about yourself?

Are there places or people that bring out the best in you?

Do you have ideas about how to use your unique gifts, passions,
and interests to help make a difference in the world?

MY FAMILY

Here we were, Father and I . . . And even though I couldn't think of anything to say, I felt myself wanting it to go on and on until the last star blinked out.

—FROM *THE SWEETNESS AT THE BOTTOM OF THE PIE*

Some of the most important moments in your life, when you learn about yourself and the world, happen with your family. At the same time, your family is also learning from YOU. Being together—living, arguing, having adventures, celebrating, hanging out, working, debating, playing, and talking—are all part of the work of a family.

Have you ever noticed how the people in your family can be your strongest advocates and loudest cheerleaders and simultaneously the most frustrating and annoying people in your life? Actually, that is one of the signs you are all growing—because conversations and events in a family change all the time.

Your family may be defined by the people who live in your house, or it may include an extended family of special people who surround you and love you.

On the next page, draw a picture or create a collage of your family or other special people in your life.

My Family

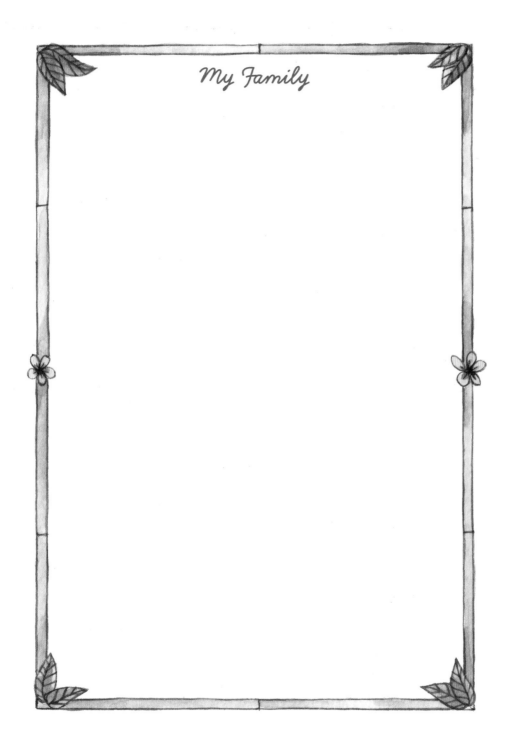

List the people in your family and the other special people in your life.
How are they important to you?

Does your family have traditions or favorite things they like to do together?

....
....
....
....
....
....
....
....
....
....
....

Do you have traditions with other special people in your life?

....
....
....
....
....
....
....
....
....
....

IDEA TO TRY: Go around the table at a family gathering and ask everyone to share the names of two adults (besides their parents) they could go to if they needed to ask an important question or share a concern. What did you learn?

Certain topics can be hard to bring up with your parents, because you feel awkward, nervous, silly, uncertain, or just plain confused. Or maybe you and your parents have completely different ideas on the subject, which then creates conflict. There are also ideas that are very easy to talk about, when you are aligned and agree on what is important or which next steps to take.

» Place a CHECK next to the topics on the next page that are tough to talk about with your parents.

» Make a STAR next to the topics that you and your parents are mostly in agreement on.

» Draw a CIRCLE around the ones you feel that you and your parents are a world apart on.

» UNDERLINE the topics you wish your parents gave you more opportunities to make your own decisions about.

How I manage my homework

Doing chores

Who I choose as my friends

Whether or not my room is clean

My grades

How often I practice an instrument

Television, movie, video game, and
music choices

Anything to do with a phone

What my hair looks like

Anything to do with puberty

Who I like/have a crush on

My obsessions/hobbies/interests

When I go to sleep and the
amount of sleep I get

How much I weigh and what
my body looks like

My day in general

Anything to do with sex

Taking a shower and wearing deodorant

What I wear

Whether or not my siblings and I are
getting along

Sleepovers and other things I do
with friends

Invitations to parties

Whether or not I am responsible

What I spend money on

How much allowance I get

Whether or not I get enough exercise
or play a sport

Being on time or being late

The amount of time I spend on
the computer

How I spend my time after school

My privacy

My manners at dinner

Trusting me more with my
own decisions

My attitude

What I am worried about

What I am afraid of

Planning for the future

IDEA TO TRY: Ask your parents to look at the list. See if
they have some of the same observations about the topics
that are easy or challenging to discuss together.

What topics of conversation feel easy and safe to discuss with your parents?

....
....
....
....
....
....
....
....
....
....
....
....
....
....
....
....

What things do you wish you could talk about more easily with your parents?

....
....
....
....
....
....
....
....
....
....
....
....
....
....

What topics are entirely off-limits because of you or your parents?

Why do you think those topics are harder to talk about?

When and where do you have your best conversations?

IDEA TO TRY: Sometimes it's easier to talk while you are side by side instead of looking at each other. Pick one of the tough topics you checked on page 33 and bring it up when you're doing something together like walking the dog or riding in the car. Notice if it was easier to talk this way.

Pick a topic that you want to discuss with your parents, but aren't confident about bringing up. Write your conversation like a play, with all of the different characters speaking their parts.

Title: ....
....

Setting: ....

Time of day: ....

Characters: ....
....
....
....
....
....

Dialogue: ....
....
....
....
....
....
....
....
....
....
....
....
....
....
....
....

How do you imagine finishing up the conversation? Do the characters
hug, apologize, walk away more peaceful or more frustrated?
Do they agree to come back to talk together again?

Now that you've written your play, do you have any new insights about how to start the conversation you want to have with your parents?

....
....
....
....
....
....
....
....
....
....
....
....
....
....
....
....
....
....
....
....
....

One of the BEST moments ever is when you feel totally and completely understood by your family—when someone really "gets" what you mean and hears what you are trying to say.

My family really understands that I am . . .

....
....
....
....
....
....
....
....
....
....
....

The thing I wish my family understood about me is . . .

....
....
....
....
....
....
....
....
....
....
....
....
....

One of the WORST moments ever is when you feel like no one in your family can see your perspective at all, and that they have absolutely no idea what it's like being you. They don't understand what you have to say.

I am pretty sure my family will never understand that I . . .

....
....
....
....
....
....
....
....
....
....
....

What do you imagine your family would wish YOU understood about THEM?

....
....
....
....
....
....
....
....
....
....
....
....
....
....

Imagine you are making a movie about your family.

What would your movie be called?

....

....

What is the plot or storyline?

....

....

....

....

....

....

Circle the style or genre of your movie.

Action	Fantasy	Other:
Adventure	Horror	....
Animated	Musical	....
Comedy	Romance	....
Documentary	Sci-fi	....
Drama	Zombie	....

Would it be set in the past, present, or future?

....

....

Would you be the star, or would someone else in your family?

....

....

Would there be a hero? A villain?

....

....

....

How would your movie end?

....

....

....

....

....

....

....

....

....

....

....

....

....

....

....

....

Make a collage of everyone's wardrobe/costumes.

Make a playlist of songs for the soundtrack.

Draw a picture of the movie poster.

Every family has moments when people don't get along. It's to be expected, because there are bound to be different opinions among people living in the same house. But when disagreements become so frequent that they seem predictable, it can feel discouraging for everyone.

How do you feel when you are not getting along with someone in your family?

When you're arguing with someone, one of the most important things you can do is to really listen and try to understand the other person's viewpoint. It's not easy, especially when you want them to agree with you.

If you could change one thing about the way your family argues, what would it be?

IDEAS TO TRY: When you find yourself in a major disagreement, try one or all of these.

1. If you've been arguing for more than two minutes, take a break and pick a time to come back together. The key is to talk it through after you both feel calmer.

2. Instead of arguing, with accusations such as "You always . . ." or "You never . . . ," use sentences that start with your own perspective and feelings, such as "I am frustrated that . . ."

3. In an argument, it can often be difficult to truly listen to the other person, because you're thinking of your next point. Repeat back to the person what they have said, so that they know they've been heard. An example: "You're frustrated because I forgot to call you."

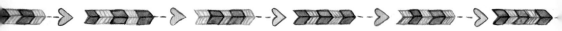

Interviewing your family and important people in your life can give you perspective beyond your own life experience.

Using the questions below and/or your own, interview a parent, grandparent, an older friend, or someone else you admire.

When you were my age . . .

» What was your favorite thing to wear?

» What were your favorite books?

» Did you have your own room? What did your bedroom look like?

» What do you remember most about school?

» Did you get an allowance from your parents?

» Did you have chores or jobs at your house?

» Did you ever travel or go places with your family?

» What did you and your friends like to do when you were together?

» Did you have a best friend?

» What did you want to be when you grew up?

» Do you remember any movies, songs, or performers that you loved?

» Did you ever feel left out or lonely?

» What were your hobbies or interests?

» What did you disagree with your parents about?

» What was it like with your siblings?

» Did you have any pets? What were they like?

» What did you look like?

» What were your favorite holiday traditions?

» Was your faith important to you?

» Who were the important people in your life outside your family?

» What do you wish someone had told you when you were a teenager?

» Is there a news event that made a significant impression on you?

» What do you want to tell me that I haven't asked

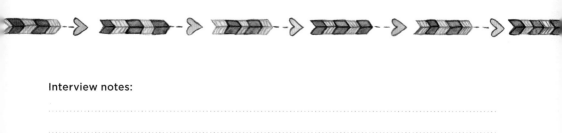

Interview notes:

More interview notes:

What did you find most interesting about the answers to your interview questions? How does the person's life compare to yours?

MY FRIENDS

*There are some things you can't share without
ending up liking each other, and knocking out a
twelve-foot mountain troll is one of them.*

—FROM *HARRY POTTER AND THE SORCERER'S STONE*

Have you noticed that some of your craziest adventures, biggest laughs, and most heartbreaking moments have been with your friends? There really is nothing like having a friend—someone to count on, argue with (and then make up with), play an imaginary game with, or plan a real-life journey with.

A friendship is a place where people feel heard and understood, challenged but secure. It's where you can try out your real self when you're away from your family. You can also learn a lot about yourself through your friendships. Even difficult friends can teach you things about yourself.

You probably have a variety of friends—some you've known your entire life, some brand-new. As in a garden, some friendships are like a small seed just getting started while others are as tall as a tree.

On the next page, draw a garden and write your
friends' names on the different plants.

My Friends

Finding people to spend time with who support and encourage you is important, but it doesn't mean that having friends is always easy.

What is the best part of HAVING a friend?

What is the hardest part about BEING a friend?

What I wish my friends understood about me:

Making new friends is a skill you will use your whole life. It is not always easy and often takes time and practice. Sometimes friendships get started more easily when you have something in common—a hobby or a passion.

Make a list of qualities that are most important to you in a friend.

What kind of friend do you want to be?

What has been your experience in making friends?

....
....
....
....
....
....
....
....
....
....
....
....
....
....
....
....
....

IDEA TO TRY: If you feel awkward starting a conversation with someone, start by asking the other person a question about themselves. Listen for things that you share in common and also things that are different, and comment on those—now you have a conversation!

Have you ever felt the need to change yourself to be friends
with someone? What was that like? How did you feel?

....
....
....
....
....
....
....
....
....
....
....
....
....
....
....
....
....
....
....
....
....
....
....
....
....

When a friendship is healthy, both people share interests and decision-making. They have good times, but they also may experience conflicts. A friendship becomes unbalanced when one friend consistently makes more compromises than the other.

Have you experienced a one-sided friendship?
How did you feel? How did you handle the situation?

Feeling IMPORTANT in a friendship means being recognized by friends for your gifts and strengths. Perhaps they noticed how you accomplished a goal, came up with a solution, or offered to help.

Describe a time your friends helped you see yourself as important.

The opposite of feeling important is when you feel embarrassed or not valued for your effort and contribution.

Describe a time you felt that friends did not understand or value your strengths.

....

....

....

....

....

....

....

....

....

....

....

....

....

....

....

....

....

IDEA TO TRY: Cut a piece of paper into strips. Write on each strip a special strength you have as a friend. Build a paper chain of these strips and hang it somewhere in your room where you will see it every day, reminding yourself of your unique qualities as a friend.

Feeling INCLUDED is when you feel acknowledged by friends as being an essential part of the group—they can't imagine the group without you being there.

Describe a time with your friends when you felt included.

....
....
....
....
....
....
....
....
....
....
....
....
....
....
....
....
....
....
....
....
....
....
....
....
....
....
....

The opposite of seeing yourself as included is feeling left out and lonely.

Describe a time when you felt left out or ignored by your friends.

....

....

....

....

....

....

....

....

....

....

....

....

....

....

....

....

....

....

....

IDEA TO TRY: With a group of friends, set a timer for five minutes and make a list of all the things that are unique about each person in the group. For example, maybe just one person has an older brother and another person doesn't watch TV—anything that makes a person different from all the others in the group.

Did you learn anything that you didn't know about your friends?

Mistakes happen in friendships. Even among good friends, feelings can get hurt and ideas can be misunderstood.

**Describe a time when you made choices that made
someone else feel left out or not valued.**

What could you have done differently?

When someone's feelings are hurt in a friendship, do you think it's easier to ask for forgiveness or to forgive someone? Why?

Have you ever had an argument with a friend that actually made the relationship stronger? What was that like?

Friendship Moments

Funniest moment:

....

....

....

....

....

....

....

Most adventurous moment:

....

....

....

....

....

....

....

Bravest moment:

....

....

....

....

....

....

....

Moment I knew my friend trusted me:

....

....

....

....

....

....

....

Moment I knew I could trust my friend:

....

....

....

....

....

....

....

Most embarrassing moment:

....

....

....

....

....

....

....

Saddest moment:

....
....
....
....
....
....
....
....

Most surprising moment:

....
....
....
....
....
....
....
....

Moment I will never forget:

....
....
....
....
....
....
....
....

Most magical moment:

....
....
....
....
....
....
....
....

Most frightening moment:

....
....
....
....
....
....
....
....

Most hopeful moment:

....
....
....
....
....
....
....
....

Talking about others is part of everyday conversation. But when you share some-one's story without their permission, it can turn into gossip and rumors. The only exception—when it is not only OK but important to share someone's story—is when you are worried about someone's safety or health.

How can you tell when everyday talk has changed into rumors and gossip?

....
....
....
....
....
....
....
....
....
....
....

How does it feel to you when people are gossiping?

....
....
....
....
....
....
....
....
....
....
....
....
....

Would all of your friends see it the same way? If not, how would some of them define gossip differently?

Describe a situation when a conversation with friends felt unsafe or when you were nervous about what people were talking about.

....
....
....
....
....
....
....
....
....
....

Sometimes people are the repeated target of hurtful words or actions by others. If this happens to you or someone else, it is important to speak up until you get the attention of an adult who can help. It takes courage to act when you are afraid, but the safety of yourself and others is a priority.

Who could you go to for help and advice?

....
....
....
....
....
....
....
....
....

List ALL the ways you could change, stop, or exit an uncomfortable conversation even if your ideas seem ridiculous, challenging, or embarrassing.

Next circle the ideas that seem the most realistic.
Then pick one and write what you can imagine saying.

Have you ever noticed that sometimes people talk about having or being a best friend almost like it's a requirement for life? Lots of girls don't have just one best friend—instead, they have several friends with whom they share different interests and activities.

What do the words BEST FRIEND mean to you?

What are some of the expectations your friends have about being a best friend? Do you think they are realistic?

....
....
....
....
....
....
....
....
....
....
....
....
....

When someone has a best friend, how does it change their other friendships? How do they interact with their best friend when in a larger group of friends?

....
....
....
....
....
....
....
....
....
....
....
....
....
....

All friendships change over time, because people change over time. Sometimes a friend moves away, or you choose to take a break from a friendship. Taking a break can give you the space you need to think about why a person is important to you or how they don't bring out the best in you.

Describe the ways your friendships have changed over your life.

....
....
....
....
....
....
....
....
....
....
....
....
....
....
....
....
....
....
....
....
....
....

Sometimes our friends become busy with other things or we grow apart. At these times it is important to be your own best friend and take care of yourself.

What are some activities you enjoy doing alone?

....

....

....

....

....

....

....

....

....

....

....

What are some activities that make you feel connected to other people in your life?

....

....

....

....

....

....

....

....

....

....

....

....

It's easier to be in a group of friends when everyone is in agreement, and it can be challenging when there are diverse opinions. Defining and standing up for what you believe in, even when it is different from the rest of the group, is an important quality of a good decision-maker.

Describe a situation where you had a different opinion or made a different choice from your friends.

Have you ever gone along with something you didn't believe in just so that you could fit in with others? What happened? How did you feel? Would you make a different choice today?

Why is it sometimes difficult to say NO to friends? What do you
put at risk when you disagree or refuse to go along?

Imagine you and some new friends are in a store shopping. You see one of the girls take a small item and put it in her bag without paying for it. All of your friends see it happen and don't say anything. What would you do?

Throughout your life there will be people who are especially interesting to you. You will find yourself thinking about them a lot, wanting to be closer emotionally and physically and to spend more time together—perhaps even more than other friends. There are a lot of ways people describe that feeling: two of them are "liking someone" or "having a crush."

What does having a crush mean to you?

Do your friends agree or disagree with you about what a crush is?
Ask three friends what they think and list their ideas.

Just because you have a crush on someone doesn't mean you need to act on your feelings right away. Building a relationship takes time, thought, and the other person's shared interest in doing the same.

Make a list of small ways that you could start to share your feelings with someone you have a crush on.

IDEA TO TRY: Ask a parent to describe a crush they had when they were young. What do they remember about how they felt? Were they embarrassed? Nervous? Excited? Did they share their feelings with the person they had a crush on, their friends, or a parent, or keep it to themselves?

Sometimes being popular means being well known or well liked by others. Other times, people are described as popular based on how they look: "Popular girls are pretty." Or how they act: "Popular girls are mean."

How is the word POPULAR used at your school or with your friends? What or who determines who is popular?

What have you noticed about people who are considered popular?

....
....
....
....
....
....
....
....
....
....
....
....
....
....
....
....
....

What does being popular mean to you?
How important is it to be thought of as popular?

....
....
....
....
....
....
....
....
....
....
....
....
....

Advice Column

Tough situations are around you every day, and sometimes YOU know just what to do. If you were the author of an advice column for girls your age, how would you answer these questions?

Write back to them sharing your best ideas.

Dear .... ,

I always feel left out. I never seem to be included in any of the conversations with other girls. There are some popular girls that I especially want to be friends with, but when I walk up to them, I notice they stop talking. Sometimes it even feels like they're talking about me. I just want to have a friend who likes me. What do I do?

From Lonely Lara

Dear Lonely Lara,

Sincerely,

Dear.. ,

My birthday is coming up, and my family has offered to throw a party in the neighborhood park so I can invite my whole class. I am super-excited and so is everyone else . . . but there's a big problem. One of the girls in my class is super-annoying. Nobody wants her to come—including me—because she always wrecks all the fun. My friends don't want me to invite her, but my mom says I have to invite everyone or skip the whole idea. Aargh, help!

From It's-My-Party Paige

Dear It's-My-Party Paige,

....

....

....

....

....

....

....

....

....

Sincerely,

....

Dear.. ,

Everyone is talking about the party this Friday, but I didn't get invited. Maybe my invitation was lost. Should I ask if I can come? I really want to go.

From Wishful Wynona

Dear Wishful Wynona,

....

....

....

....

....

....

....

....

....

....

....

....

Sincerely,

....

Dear... ,

I have a friend who seems to like me, but sometimes when we're talking she says something to criticize the way I look or how I dress. The other day she even said she thought I was fat. When I speak up about it, she always says the same thing: "I was just kidding! Can't you tell it's a joke?" I don't know what to think sometimes. What can I say to her?

From Confused Claire

Dear Confused Claire,

....

....

....

....

....

....

....

....

....

....

Sincerely,

....

MY FEELINGS

*So, this is my life. And I want you to know
that I am both happy and sad and I'm still trying
to figure out how that could be.*

—FROM *THE PERKS OF BEING A WALLFLOWER*

As you are growing up, it can sometimes feel like you have a million emotions at once. Some feelings last for days, and some only for a moment. It can be confusing when you feel sad one minute and the next you are laughing out loud, or when you act mad when you are actually afraid.

Feelings—our emotions—are an important part of who we are. They start in our brains and send messages to other parts of our bodies to create strong physical reactions, like tears, sweat, laughter, or a red face.

Recognizing your feelings is a key part of growing up. People who manage their emotions well have stronger decision-making and friendship skills. When you are tuned in to your emotions, feel confident about expressing them, and use them to help you effectively communicate, then you have some essential tools in your toolbox for life.

On the next page, draw or make a collage showing a series
of faces with each of the emotions you had today.

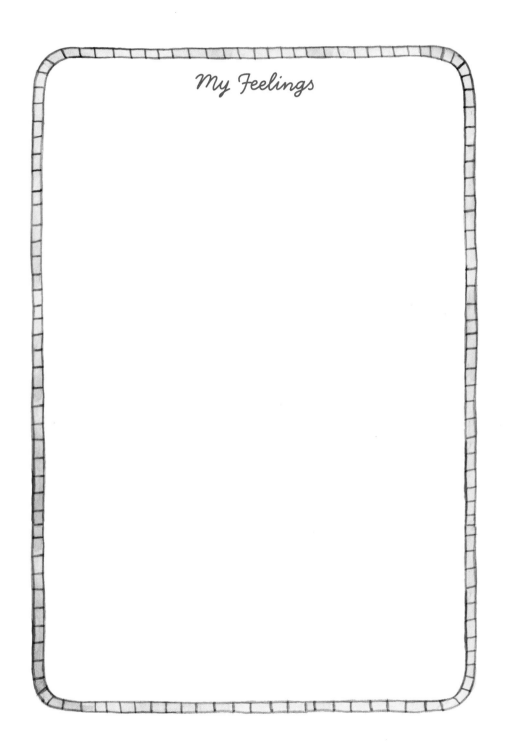

My Feelings

When you experience uncomfortable feelings, it can seem like you are supposed to ignore them or push them aside, as if feelings are bad or wrong. But actually, by paying attention to your emotions, you learn more about your motivations, obstacles, passions, and values.

Pay attention for an entire day and circle all the emotions you've felt:

Afraid	Fascinated	Nervous
Angry	Focused	On top of the world
Anxious	Foolish	Overwhelmed
Astonished	Frustrated	Pressured
Awake	Glad	Questioning
Beautiful	Grateful	Relieved
Blessed	Guilty	Resigned
Bored	Happy	Resilient
Busy	Helpful	Restless
Capable	Hopeful	Sad
Charmed	Hopeless	Shocked
Clever	Hungry	Startled
Committed	Hurt	Stressed
Concerned	Ignored	Strong
Confused	In love	Stupid
Determined	Jealous	Surprised
Discouraged	Joyful	Tense
Disgusted	Kind	Trapped
Eager	Left out	Troubled
Electrified	Lonely	Ugly
Engaged	Loved	Uncertain
Enthusiastic	Loyal	Valued
Excited	Mad	Worried

You CAN'T have a lot of control over which feelings show up, but you CAN control what actions and words you use to communicate them—and you can learn to manage them skillfully. In fact, you can also learn to wait to act on your feelings in order to have time to think things through.

Pick two or three of the feelings you circled and describe what you did in the moment when you had those feelings.

Stress can affect your body, sleep, appetite, and ability to concentrate. You may feel your stress increase when something is new, or when you are afraid, or when you are not in control of a situation.

Circle the situations that make you anxious or stressed.

Being late

Getting lost

Making a hard decision

Not being invited

Being teased

Feeling ignored

When an adult is angry

Getting in trouble

Being in the dark

Getting a bad grade

Performing in an important concert or recital

Playing in a championship game

When something doesn't go well

When a friend is hurt

When someone is sick

When someone is sad

When you get hurt

When someone wants you to do something dangerous

When someone wants you to do something against the rules

Being alone

When a growling animal is nearby

Trying something new

The first day of school or camp or anything

When you haven't done your best

When you've made a mistake or get in trouble

IDEA TO TRY: Ask a friend or parent what makes them stressed out. Compare the lists. Are there similarities? What do they do when they feel that way?

Make a list of things that create the most stress in your life.

What do you notice about the things that cause stress for you?

What expectations do you have of yourself that cause you to feel stressed?

....

....

....

....

....

....

....

....

....

....

....

....

....

**What expectations do others, like teachers and
parents, have that make you feel stressed?**

....

....

....

....

....

....

....

....

....

....

....

....

....

What other responsibilities or relationships do you feel worried or concerned about?

....
....
....
....
....
....
....
....
....
....
....
....
....
....
....
....
....
....
....
....
....
....
....
....
....

IDEA TO TRY: Using a calendar, keep track of the days and times you feel stressed. Make notes about what you do to calm your mind and body. You might write in a journal, talk to someone, exercise, meditate, or listen to music. What are some other ideas?

Anger can be a powerful emotion. It can come as a response to someone treating you or another person badly, or as a reaction to someone behaving in a surprising and disappointing way. Anger can also be used to inflict pain and gain power over others in a destructive way. When anger goes unchecked and uncontrolled, people get hurt.

**Remember a time you were very angry about something.
Describe how your body and mind felt in the moment.**

....
....
....
....
....
....
....
....
....
....

When I am angry with SOMEONE, I feel . . .

....
....
....
....
....
....
....
....
....
....

When I am angry with MYSELF, I feel . . .

....
....
....
....
....
....
....
....
....
....
....
....
....

What does it feel like when someone is mad at YOU?

....
....
....
....
....
....
....
....
....
....
....
....
....
....

Anger can lead to positive outcomes, if you use your anger to create change for yourself or someone else.

What are some ways you can picture turning something that makes you mad into a positive change for yourself or someone else?

Some people have turned their frustration into a commitment to make the world a better place.

**Are there ways you can picture turning what angers
you into a change for your community?**

....
....
....
....
....
....
....
....
....
....
....
....
....
....
....
....
....

IDEA TO TRY: To channel your energy, find a local organization that supports an important cause. Are you angry about the environment? Organize a neighborhood cleanup. Are you mad about world hunger? Collect food for your local food bank. Are you just plain mad? Find someone who can use your help in a simple way.

Everyone experiences sadness. Often people feel sad when there is a major change in their family, when they lose something they treasure, or when they feel like they've been mistreated. When you are sad, it can affect the whole way you view the world.

Draw a picture showing the color and shape of *sad*. Add some lyrics of a song or describe a sound that defines sadness best to you.

When you are sad, what words are helpful to hear from others? What words are not helpful?

Describe a time you pretended to be happy when actually you were sad.
Why do you think that happened?

....
....
....
....
....
....
....
....
....
....
....
....
....
....

Talking things over can help you through a difficult time.
Make a list of people you trust to share your thoughts with when you feel sad.

....
....
....
....
....
....
....
....
....
....
....
....
....
....

What makes you happy and joyful can come from a variety of different experiences. Being happy can mean feeling relaxed and peaceful, relieved and satisfied, or excited with anticipation.

Write about a time when you were bursting with happy feelings.

....
....
....
....
....
....
....
....
....
....

Are there certain people, places, or moments that bring out happy feelings in you?

....
....
....
....
....
....
....
....
....

What are ways that you have created a happy experience for someone else?

IDEA TO TRY: Start a "favorite things" list to have on hand on a rough day. Are there favorite movies that make you laugh out loud? Songs that always make you smile? Books that inspire you? People who are good listeners and always cheer you up?

MY BODY

I am not pretty. I am not beautiful.
I am as radiant as the sun.

—FROM *THE HUNGER GAMES*

Your body is one of the most fascinating parts of who you are—especially during puberty. Within just a few years, puberty transforms a girl's body into a woman's in size, shape, and function.

Every girl has her own unique experience of puberty. How fast or slow you go through the process, and the size and shape you will become, are largely determined by your biological parents and your health. However, across time and around the globe, all girls experience the same things: growing taller; putting on weight; growing breasts, and underarm and pubic hair; getting body odor; and starting a period.

Girls in puberty often feel self-conscious about their changing bodies—uncertain of how it's all going to work out. But thinking through the experience can give you helpful insights into the whole puberty thing.

On the next page, draw a picture or create a
collage of yourself as an adult.

Adult Me

The Whole Puberty Thing

Check the boxes that describe how you feel about puberty:

☐ I know everything I need to know about puberty.

☐ I have a few questions.

☐ Will everything turn out OK?

☐ Why is puberty so hard?

☐ Why are we talking about this?

☐ I've been looking forward to it my whole life.

☐ It's my worst nightmare.

☐ I feel confused.

☐ I feel anxious.

☐ I feel excited.

☐ I wish it would start today.

☐ I wish it would end today.

☐ I am excited about growing taller but not about anything else.

More feelings: ....

....

....

....

....

....

....

....

....

....

....

....

....

....

....

....

....

....

What parts of puberty are you most looking forward to?
What are you least looking forward to?

Most: ....

....

....

....

Least: ....

....

....

....

What advice would you give another girl about puberty
that you have found particularly helpful?

....

....

....

....

....

....

....

....

What questions do you still have about puberty?

....

....

....

....

....

....

....

You may notice that you have different feelings, physically and emotionally, around the time of your period.

What are the best things you can do to take care of yourself physically and emotionally around your period?

There are MYTHS and TRUTHS about what girls experience during puberty. Some of these ideas have been passed down through generations. Below is a list of these myths and truths—see if you can tell the difference.

Circle the numbers of the TRUTHS. The answers are below.

1. Girls should not wash their hair while having a period.

2. The size and shape of your breasts will change throughout your life.

3. Girls should not play basketball or dance while having a period.

4. Bras are a requirement for all girls with breasts.

5. Body odor comes from sweat mixed with bacteria and air.

6. Washing your face more will guarantee fewer pimples.

7. Body odor is unnatural.

8. Most people get pimples.

9. Girls shouldn't swim during their periods.

10. Being in water makes your period worse.

11. Exercise can be helpful in managing cramps.

12. Some women believe they are more creative and energized when they are having their periods.

13. You look different when you have your period.

14. Once you shave your legs, the hair will forever be changed and you will always have to shave them.

15. Girls stop growing the day they start their periods.

TRUTHS: 2, 5, 8, 11, 12

IDEA TO TRY: Keep track of how your body feels right before your period, during your period, and after your period.

Do you have a lot of energy, or are you more tired? Do you experience cramps or a headache, or do you feel especially strong and powerful?

Also keep track of your emotions around your period. What do you notice about how your moods change? Is there a pattern?

Your body needs to be recharged by sleep to allow it to grow well during puberty and to keep your mind rested. Typically, a girl between the ages of eight and fifteen needs about ten hours of sleep a night.

Do you ever have trouble sleeping? What helps you get a good night's sleep?

How do you feel if you don't get enough sleep?

....
....
....
....
....
....
....
....
....
....
....
....
....
....
....
....
....

IDEA TO TRY: Using a calendar, keep track of how many hours of sleep you get each night. Make notes about how you feel when you wake up and throughout each day.

When your body is in middle of the transformation project called puberty, it is especially important to fuel it with good food that builds bones, muscles, and brain cells.

Read the list below and circle the foods that you eat most days.

IRON. Important for growing bodies, especially during your period.
Some sources: Meat, fish, chicken, lentils, broccoli, bok choy, spinach, soybeans

PROTEIN. Important for growing bodies and muscle development.
Some sources: Meat, poultry, fish, tofu, eggs, nuts, quinoa, beans, lentils, dairy products

CALCIUM. Important for bone strength.
Some sources: Dairy products, dark-green leafy vegetables, nuts

VITAMINS & NUTRIENTS. Important for healthy digestion, energy, and strength, and to give your body essential ingredients to defend itself against illness.
Some sources: A variety of fruits and vegetables, whole grains

UNSATURATED FATS. Important as an energy and calorie source.
Some sources: Oils (peanut, canola, and olive), nuts, avocados

ENOUGH CALORIES. Important to sustain your body's growth, and to fuel the sports, activities, and thinking you do every day.

WATER. Important as an alternative to sugary drinks—to replace the water your body loses in sweat and urine, and to keep your cells healthy.

What snacks could you eat every day that include some
of the important ingredients from this list?

....

....

....

....

....

....

....

....

....

Make a list of your favorite snacks or draw a picture of your favorite meal.

What are family meals like at your house?

....

....

....

....

....

....

....

....

....

IDEA TO TRY: Keep track of what you eat for a day or two. What do you notice about how your feelings affect your eating? When you are stressed, do you find that you eat differently? What about when you are tired or nervous? What kinds of foods do you choose as your moods change—do you make healthier choices at certain times more than others?

Beauty isn't just what you look like on the outside. True beauty comes from the inside. Being your best self—sharing your gifts, following your passions, and building friendships—is where it all begins.

Have you ever been with a group of girls who are talking negatively about their bodies? Describe the conversation.

....

....

....

....

....

....

....

....

....

....

Why do you think this type of conversation happens when some girls get together?

....

....

....

....

....

....

....

....

....

....

....

....

....

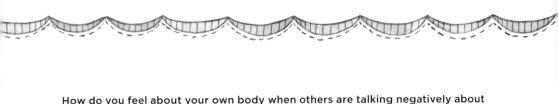

How do you feel about your own body when others are talking negatively about theirs or are being judgmental about someone else's?

When you stop to think about it, your body is working twenty-four hours a day, giving you the ability to run, do science experiments, write poetry, or sing. To follow your passions and interests. Your body is actually quite amazing.

What I LIKE about my body:

....

....

....

....

....

....

....

....

....

....

....

What I APPRECIATE about my body:

....

....

....

....

....

....

....

....

....

....

....

....

....

What I wish were different:

....
....
....
....
....
....
....
....
....
....

Do you find yourself more often critical of or grateful for your body?
Why do you think that's the case?

....
....
....
....
....
....
....
....
....
....
....
....
....

What I CAN change about my body:

....
....
....
....
....
....
....
....
....
....
....
....

What I CANNOT change about my body:

....
....
....
....
....
....
....
....
....
....
....

Write about a time when you felt your body was perfect
for what you wanted to do in that moment.

....
....
....
....
....
....
....
....
....
....
....
....
....
....
....
....
....
....
....
....
....
....
....

IDEA TO TRY: Poetry can sometimes say things that can't be captured in paragraphs or pictures. The beauty of a poem is that it can be long or short, rhyming or not rhyming, simple or complicated. Write a poem about how you are feeling or where you are in your life.

About the Author and This Journal

JULIE METZGER, RN, MN, has worked for more than twenty-five years with families of preteens and teens on topics of puberty, sexuality, and decision-making. Bringing a wealth of knowledge from her experiences as a pediatric nurse and a parent of three young adults, Metzger is a well-respected and popular speaker.

Metzger advocates for adolescents and families in the community through Great Conversations. She authored a book for preteens, *Will Puberty Last My Whole Life?* with cofounder, Dr. Rob Lehman. For more, visit GreatConversations.com.

This journal was inspired by thousands of girls and their parents who have shared their questions, stories, worries, and hopes in Metzger's Great Conversations classes over the past two decades. Many of the ideas in this journal came from real girls who were brave enough to ask their questions out loud and explore them with each other.